# I Can Add,
# It's Not So Bad!

**Tracy Kompelien**

Consulting Editors, Diane Craig, M.A./Reading Specialist
and Susan Kosel, M.A. Education

Published by ABDO Publishing Company, 4940 Viking Drive, Edina, Minnesota 55435.

Printed in the United States.

Credits
Edited by: Pam Price
Curriculum Coordinator: Nancy Tuminelly
Cover and Interior Design and Production: Mighty Media
Photo Credits: ShutterStock, Wewerka Photography

Library of Congress Cataloging-in-Publication Data

Kompelien, Tracy, 1975-
    I can add, it's not so bad! / Tracy Kompelien
    p. cm. -- (Math made fun)
    ISBN 10 1-59928-513-4 (hardcover)
    ISBN 10 1-59928-514-2 (paperback)

    ISBN 13 978-1-59928-513-9 (hardcover)
    ISBN 13 978-1-59928-514-6 (paperback)
    1. Addition--Juvenile literature. I. Title. II. Series.

QA115.K66 2007
513.2'11--dc22

                                                        2006015297

### SandCastle Level: Transitional

SandCastle™ books are created by a professional team of educators, reading specialists, and content developers around five essential components—phonemic awareness, phonics, vocabulary, text comprehension, and fluency—to assist young readers as they develop reading skills and strategies and increase their general knowledge. All books are written, reviewed, and leveled for guided reading, early reading intervention, and Accelerated Reader® programs for use in shared, guided, and independent reading and writing activities to support a balanced approach to literacy instruction. The SandCastle™ series has four levels that correspond to early literacy development. The levels help teachers and parents select appropriate books for young readers.

| **Emerging Readers** | **Beginning Readers** | **Transitional Readers** | **Fluent Readers** |
|:---:|:---:|:---:|:---:|
| (no flags) | (1 flag) | (2 flags) | (3 flags) |

These levels are meant only as a guide. All levels are subject to change.

# To add

is to put two or more numbers together to find a total number, or sum.

Words used to talk about adding:
**count**
**equals**
**equation**
**how many**
**plus**
**sum**

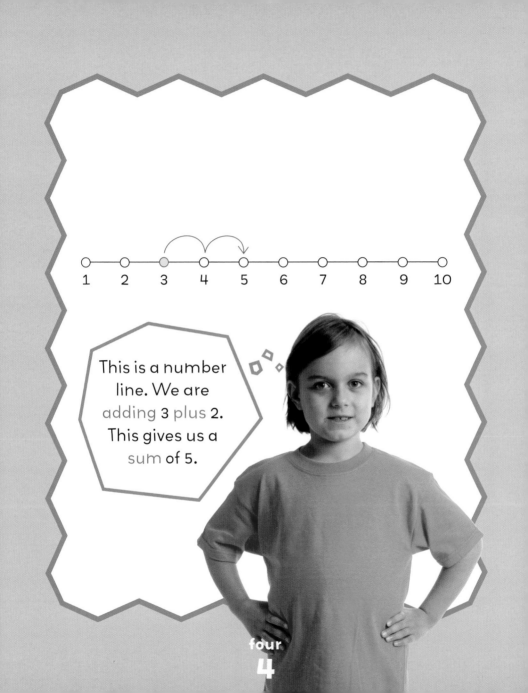

This is a number line. We are adding 3 plus 2. This gives us a sum of 5.

The ◯ is on the 3.

I count forward 2 places.

When I add 2 to 3,

the sum I get is 5.

3 + 2 = 5

plus      equals    sum

# I can show addition with an equation, or addition sentence.

I know that this is an addition sentence because I am using the plus sign and the equal sign to find the sum.

eight
8

I see that there are 3 bees.
I add 3 plus 2 and the sum is 5.

# I Can Add, It's Not So Bad!

Tad's dad

wants him to add.

So he adds his toys

on a large, yellow        .

I will figure out
how many
toys I have
by counting to
find the sum.

**twelve**
**12**

A  and a are the first toys to add.

Tad writes the sum down on his pad.

I have 1 cow plus 1 fish. The sum of the toys is 2.

$1 + 1 = 2$

fourteen
**14**

Then he adds a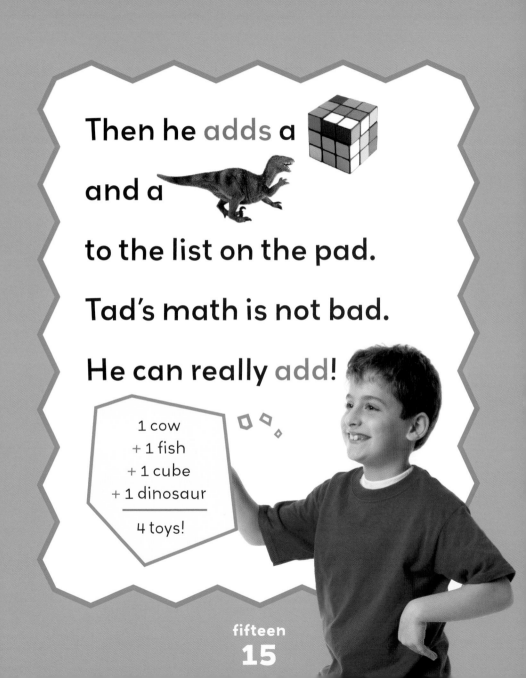

and a

to the list on the pad.

Tad's math is not bad.

He can really add!

1 cow
+ 1 fish
+ 1 cube
+ 1 dinosaur
_____
4 toys!

# Adding Every Day!

I see **3** cubs plus **1** lion. The sum of the animals is **4**.

$3 + 1 = 4$

**1** tiger has been added. Now there are **5** animals.

$4 + 1 = 5$

twenty
**20**

1 monkey and 1 bird have been added. Now I have more than before.

$5 + 2 = 7$

# When you go to the zoo, can you add the animals you see?

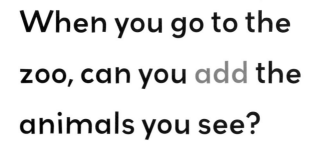

The answer I get is the sum. The sum is the biggest number in an addition sentence.

$1 + 1 + 1 = 3$

# Glossary

**count** – to add numbers one at a time.

**equal** – having exactly the same amount.

**equation** – a number sentence.

**plus** – in addition to.

**sum** – the answer to an addition problem.